THE SUPERNATURAL POWER OF PROPHECY

For no prophecy recorded in Scripture was ever thought up by the prophet himself. It was the Holy Spirit within these godly men who gave them true messages from God.

2 Peter 1:21 *TLB*

by
Franklin N. Abazie

The Supernatural Power of Prophecy
COPYRIGHT 2016 BY Franklin N Abazie
ISBN: 978-1-94513308-4

All right reserved. This book or any portion thereof may not be reproduced or used in any manner whatsoever without the express written permission of the publisher, except for the use of brief quotations in a book review. All Bible quotes are from King James Version and others as noted.

Published by: F N ABAZIE PUBLISHING HOUSE—aka, Empowerment Bookstore

That I may publish with the voice of thanksgiving and tell of all thy wondrous works.
Psalms 26:7

To order additional copies, wholesales or booking call:
the Church office (973-372-7518)
or Empowerment Bookstore Hotline (973-393-8518)

Worship address:
343 Sanford Avenue, Newark, New Jersey 07106
Administrative Head Office address:
33 Schley Street Newark New Jersey 07112
Email: pastorfranknto@yahoo.com
Website www.fnabaziehealingministries.org
Publishing House: www.fnabaziepublishinghouse.org

This book is a production of F N Abazie Publishing House. A publication Arms of Miracle of God Ministries 2016.
First Edition

CONTENTS

THE MANDATE OF THE COMMISSION......................iv
ARMS OF THE COMMISSION..v
INTRODUCTION..vi
CHAPTER 1
Who Is a Prophet..1
CHAPTER 2
The Mysteries of the Prophetic Word...................20
CHAPTER 3
Engaging the Prophetic Word...............................25
CHAPTER 4
Prayer of Salvation...52
CHAPTER 5
About the Author..59

THE MANDATE OF THE COMMISSION

"The moment is due to impact your world through the revival of the healing & miracle ministry of Jesus Christ of Nazareth.

"I am sending you to restore health unto thee and I will heal thee of thy wounds, said the Lord of Host."

ARMS OF THE COMMISSION

1) F N Abazie Ministries—Miracle of God Ministries (Miracle Chapel Intl)

2) F N Abazie TV Ministries: Global Television Ministry Outreach

3) F N Abazie Radio Ministries: Radio Broadcasting Outreach

4) F N Abazie Publishing House: Book Publication

5) F N Abazie Bible School: also called Word of Healing Bible School (W.O.H.B.S.)

6) F N Abazie Evangelistic Ass: Miracle of God Ministries: Global Crusade

7) Empowerment Bookstore: Book distribution

8) F N Abazie Helping Hands: Meeting the Help of the Needy Worldwide

9) F N Abazie Disaster Recovery Mission: Global Disaster Recovery

10) F N Abazie Prison Ministry: Prison Ministry For All Convicts "Second Chance"

Some of our ministry arms are awaiting the appointed time to commence.

INTRODUCTION

Despise not prophesyings.
1 Thessalonians 5:20

Without reservation, prophecy has always drawn strong opposition and criticism because of its nature. There has always been strong opposition and contention concerning the prophetic ministry. Even from the days of Jeremiah, Isaiah, Zecheriah, Zerubabel, Nathan the prophet and a few others, etc. The word of prophecy has always drawn strong criticism and oppositions from all aspect of life.

I will raise them up a Prophet from among their brethren, like unto thee, and will put my words in his mouth; and he shall speak unto them all that I shall command him.
Deuteronomy 18:18

As A MAN OF GOD who operates in the office of a PROPHET, I love to clarify lots of Prevailing Argument that has hindered us from experiencing gift of the prophet and his prophetic ministry.

Knowing this first, that no prophecy of the scripture is of any private interpretation.
2 Peter 1:20

All prophesies comes from THE HOLY SPIRIT.
Now the Lord is that Spirit: and where
the Spirit of the Lord is, there is liberty.
2 Corinthians 3:18

For the prophecy came not in old time by
the will of man: but holy men of God spake
as they were moved by the Holy Ghost.
2 Peter 1:21

All prophecies comes from the Lord.

Although God speaks to us all in diverse ways, but most of us always want a human agent (the prophet) to rehearse it to our hearing before we can confirm it. Almost everybody these days is a prophet. Some folks have covenanted with familiar spirits just to have the ability to prophesy. "I have not sent these prophets, *yet they ran: I have not spoken to them, yet they prophesied."* (Jeremiah 23:21)

Thus saith the Lord of hosts, Hearken not unto the words
of the prophets that prophesy unto you:
they make you vain: they speak a vision
of their own heart, and not out of
the mouth of the Lord.
Jeremiah 23:16

This misconception about the spoken word of a prophet of God must be double checked and corrected. *"I have heard what the prophets said, that prophesy lies in my name, saying, I have dreamed, I have dreamed. How long shall this be in the heart of the prophets that prophesy lies? yea, they are prophets of the deceit of their own heart."* (Jeremiah 23:25-26)

> *When a prophet speaketh in the name of the Lord,*
> *if the thing follow not, nor come to pass,*
> *that is the thing which the Lord hath not spoken,*
> *but the prophet hath spoken it presumptuously:*
> *thou shalt not be afraid of him.*
> **Deuteronomy 18:22**

This wrong perception has so much drawned prevailing argument about the "prophetic ministry." So many of us who were not called into the prophetic ministry has entered the prophetic ministry, simply because it attracts the people of God. It brings comfort, release, and understanding. *"Behold, I am against the prophets, saith the Lord, that use their tongues, and say, He saith."* (Jeremiah 23:31)

Besides the prophet of God, God speaks to us through the written word of the Bible, through our dreams, revelations and visions. It is my desire in this book to balance what you perhaps already have some relevant information about.

Over the years, most of us have misinterpreted and misrepresented the **p**rophet and his ministry. The prophetic ministry is not a new age doctrine. It is not knew at all, at least to my Nigerian people, we must therefore pay close attention to details concerning the PROHETIC MINISTRY. I have seen married couples depend on the PROPHESIED WORD OF GOD until there was no other alternative to their predicament. "For God hath not given us the spirit of fear; but of power, and of love, and of a sound mind".2timothy1:7.we all are absolutely responsible for "THE OUTCOME OF OUR LIVES."

Behold, I am against them that prophesy false dreams, saith the Lord, and do tell them, and cause my people to err by their lies, and by their lightness; yet I sent them not, nor commanded them: therefore they shall not profit this people at all, saith the Lord."
Jeremiah 23:32

And as for the prophet, and the priest, and the people, that shall say, The burden of the Lord, I will even punish that man and his house.
Jeremiah 23:34

I believe we are all in support of the prophetic ministry. Therefore come with me as we bring a teaching, with revelation that will clarify lots of bugging unanswered areas of the prophetic ministry.

HAPPY READING!

THE PROPHETIC WORD FROM THE LORD FOR THE YEAR 2016

Although I have had so many great prophecies over the years from the Lord, below is the prophetic word from the Lord for the year 2016 that is also written on my Facebook page.

On December 31st, 2015, at about 7:53pm in the evening, the Holy Spirit came to me and began speaking to me the following prophetic words—

"Thus saidth the Lord—2016 is The Lord's Year of Supernatural Release. All those imprisoned and those in shackles shall be released by the Spirit of the Living God. A few earthquakes in California and a few strange places. Donald Trump the surprise of the Republican Party. Obama releasing a few prisoners.

"A new immune disease attacking the human race. CDC. take note. Flood Again in Asaba region of Nigeria. Wild fire in Igboland. Nigerians are in shambles as the economy deteriorates. Brussels and Antwerp, Belgium the hot zone for terrorists in 2016. One well-known organization headquarters burning down. Thus said the Lord. Buhari's last term in office complicated with liver and lung disease. Prayers, supplications and intercession be made to God in Heaven for quick intervention. Thus saidth the Lord."

Among those prophecies, below are a number of the spoken words from the Lord that have been fulfiled:

—Zika virus break out is a fulfilment of the above prophetic word from the Lord. Recall...

> *"A new immune disease attacking the human race. CDC, take note."*

—The terrorist attack on the Brussels airport in March 2016 is a fulfilment of the above prophetic word from the Lord.

> *"Brussels and Antwerp, Belgium the hot zone for terrorists in 2016."*

—Donald Trump running as a candidate for the Republican party is a fulfilment of the above prophetic word from the Lord.

"Donald Trump the surprise of the Republican Party."

—Obama plans to release a few prisoners before he leaves the office of the President of the United States of America.

> *"Obama releasing a few prisoners."*

—Every word from the Lord must surely come to pass.

It may take time, but it will surely be fulfiled.
*For the vision is yet for an appointed time,
but at the end it shall speak, and not lie: though it tarry,
wait for it; because it will surely come, it will not tarry.*
Habakkuk 2:3

As long we are in one communion with the Holy Spirit, God will speak and we shall hear. It takes the Holy Spirit to activate the power of the prophetic ministry.

CONFIRMED WORD OF PROPHESY

The prophetic word from the Lord from me has been tried, although it tarried, but it surely came to pass. There has been a strong prophetic word from the Lord that came with specific dates about a missing teenager who was supposed to be found on a specific date. On the prophesied date, the prophesied word tarried until about 10:55pm, when the police confirmed that the teenage girl who was missing for about five days had been found. As far as I know, GOD cannot lie.

For I am the Lord: I will speak, and the word that I shall speak shall come to pass; it shall be no more prolonged: for in your days, O rebellious house, will I say the word, and will perform it, saith the Lord God.
Ezekiel 12:25

*Therefore say unto them, Thus saith the Lord God;
There shall none of my words be prolonged any more,
but the word which I have spoken shall be done,
saith the Lord God.*
Ezekiel 12:28

WE MUST RESPECT THE HOLY SPIRIT IF WE DESIRE TO HEAR FROM THE THRONE ROOM OF HEAVEN

*The Holy Spirit is God, He is an advocate and
a representative of the supreme sovereign power of
God. As a care taker and representative. For in him we
live, and move, and have our being; as certain also of
your own poets have said, For we are also his offspring.*
Acts 17:20

IT IS THE HOLY SPIRIT THAT REVEALS TO THE PROPHET

*The secret things belong unto the Lord our God:
but those things which are revealed belong unto us
and to our children for ever, that we may do
all the words of this law.*
Deuteronomy 29:29

*Howbeit when he, the Spirit of truth, is come, he will
guide you into all truth: for he shall not speak of himself;
but whatsoever he shall hear, that shall he speak:
and he will shew you things to come.*

John 16:13
AS LONG AS WE ARE IN THE SPIRIT, THE HOLY SPIRIT SHOWS US THINGS TO COME—OUR FUTURE

But the natural man receiveth not the things of the Spirit of God: for they are foolishness unto him: neither can he know them, because they are spiritually discerned.
1 Corinthians 2:14

THE HOLY SPIRIT MAKES INTERCESSION FOR US BEFORE THE FATHER

Likewise the Spirit also helpeth our infirmities: for we know not what we should pray for as we ought: but the Spirit itself maketh intercession for us with groanings which cannot be uttered.
Romans 8:26

For the prophecy came not in old time by the will of man: but holy men of God spake as they were moved by the Holy Ghost.
2 Peter 1:21

HIS DESTINY WAS THE CROSS....

HIS PURPOSE WAS LOVE....

HIS REASON WAS YOU....

For the testimony of Jesus is the spirit of prophecy.
Revelation 19:11

HIGHLIGHTS

HOW TO OPERATE IN THE PROPHETIC

REPENTANCE

Although so many fake prophets have entered the church of God, every genuine prophet of God must be a man/woman who have genuinely repented the gift of the Holy Spirit will not be established for utterance unless we humble ourselves, forsake our sins, and seek his face.

If my people, which are called by my name, shall humble themselves, and pray, and seek my face, and turn from their wicked ways; then will I hear from heaven, and will forgive their sin, and will heal their land.
2 Chronicles 7:14

Then Peter said unto them, Repent, and be baptized every one of you in the name of Jesus Christ for the remission of sins, and ye shall receive the gift of the Holy Ghost.
Acts 2:38

FAITH

We having the same spirit of faith, according as it is written, I believed, and therefore have I spoken; we also believe, and therefore speak.
2 Corinthians 4:13

It takes the SPIRIT OF FAITH to operate in the prophetic. The bible says Yea, a man may say, Thou hast faith, and I have works: shew me thy faith without thy works, and I will shew thee my faith by my works.
James 2:18

HUMILITY

Every man of the Spirit is a humble man/woman of God. It takes humility to comprehend the dynamics of the Spirit of God. The reason Moses could hear directly from God was because he was a very humble man. *"Now the man Moses was very meek, above all the men which were upon the face of the earth."* (Numbers 12:3) *"And the Lord said unto Moses, I will do this thing also that thou hast spoken: for thou hast found grace in my sight, and I know thee by name."* (Exodus 33:17) As long as we are PROUD, GOD will resist from SPEAKING to us.

REMEMBER...

"But he giveth more grace. Wherefore he saith, God resisteth the proud, but giveth grace unto the humble." (James 4:6)

PRAYER

But ye beloved, building up your selves on your most holy faith, praying in the Holy Ghost.
Jude 1:20

Every prophet/prophetess of God must be a man/woman of prayer. He/she must be a man/woman of the Spirit. *"But the natural man receiveth not the things of the Spirit of God: for they are foolishness unto him: neither can he know them, because they are spiritually discerned."* (1 Corinthians 2:14)

Every time we pray, we depend on the holy spirit. The Bible says *"Likewise the Spirit also helpeth our infirmities; for we know not what we should pray for as we ought: but the Spirit itself maketh intercession for us with groaning which cannot be uttered."* (Romans 8:26) Every time we **pray** we move the Holy Spirit into action.

For the prophecy came not in old time by the will of man: but holy men of God spake as they were moved by the Holy Ghost.
2 Peter 1:21

PRAYER POINT TO ACTIVATE THE PRESENCE OF THE HOLY SPIRIT

1) Holy Spirit, reveal yourself to me, in the name of Jesus.

2) Holy Spirit, crush every daily habit of sin, in the name of Jesus.

3) Holy Spirit, become my companion today, in the name of Jesus.

4) Holy Spirit, grant me access, in the name of Jesus.

5) Power of God, grant me the GRACE to live right for Jesus Christ.

6) Hand of God, deliver me from sin, in the name of Jesus.

7) Fire of God, burn every sinful thoughts from my mind, in the name of Jesus.

8) I proclaim authority over every prevailing sin in my life, in Jesus name.

9) I destroy every root of sin in my life, in Jesus name.

10) Sin shall not have dominion over my life, in the name of Jesus.

11) Lord God, emphasize genuine repentance over my spirit man, in the name of Jesus

12) Holy Spirit, revive and rekindle your fire of revival inside of me, in the name of Jesus.

13) Power of God, hijack the controlling forces oppressing my life, in the name of Jesus.

14) Blood of Jesus, take over my life, in the name of Jesus.

15) O Lord, baptize me with the gift of the Holy Spirit.

16) Holy Spirit, breathe afresh upon my life, in the name of Jesus.

17) Holy Spirit, take possession of my will, in the name of Jesus.

18) Holy Spirit, make yourself real to me, in the name of Jesus.

19) Holy Spirit, fan your revival fire upon my life, in the name of Jesus.

KEEP IN MIND…

For he that speaketh in an unknown tongue speaketh not unto men, but unto God: for no man understandeth him; howbeit in the spirit he speaketh mysteries.

But he that prophesieth speaketh unto men to edification, and exhortation, and comfort.

He that speaketh in an unknown tongue edifieth himself; but he that prophesieth edifieth the church.
1 Corianthians 14:2-4

CHAPTER 1
WHO IS A PROPHET?

A prophet is God's spokesman. There is no gender difference—meaning if he is a man, he is called a prophet, and if she is a woman she is called a prophetess. They are God's representative who reveals and speaks for God concerning the life of man on earth. As God's oracle prophets/prophetesses reveal and give us warning from God. They reveal to us about our past, present and warnings reveal and alert us of the future. Prophets, therefore, are God's agents of solution for all our frustration. *"Surely the Lord God will do nothing, but he revealeth his secret unto his servants the prophets."* (Amos 3:7)

Prophets therefore are agents of God's solution for man's situation.

Who is he that saith, and it cometh to pass, when the Lord commandeth it not?
Lamentations 3:37

GOD MUST BE THE ONE SPEAKING THROUGH US—OTHERWISE IT WILL NOT COME TO PASS

For I am the Lord: I will speak, and the word that I shall speak shall come to pass; it shall be no more prolonged: for in your days, O rebellious house, will I say the word, and will perform it, saith the Lord God.
Ezekial 12:25

Therefore say unto them, Thus saith the Lord God; There shall none of my words be prolonged any more, but the word which I have spoken shall be done, saith the Lord God.
Ezekial 12:28

WHAT ARE THE FUNCTIONS OF A PROPHET?

1) PROPHETS ARE AGENTS OF WARNING & REVELATION

Although God warns and reveals all things to us daily, a lot of us are ignorant and neglects god's warning and revelations. *"For God speaketh once, yea twice, yet man perceiveth it not. In a dream, in a vision of the night, when deep sleep falleth upon men, in slumberings upon the bed; Then he openeth the ears of men, and sealeth their instruction."* (Job 33:14-16)

Noah, as a prophet of God during his dispensation, moved with fear, because he was warned of God. *"By faith Noah, being warned of God of things not seen as yet, moved with fear, prepared an ark to the saving of his house; by the he condemned the world, and became heir of the righteousness which is by faith."* (Hebrews 11:7)

Every Prophet/Prophetess of God os God's agent of warning and revelation. *"Son of man, I have made thee a watchman unto the house of Israel: therefore hear the word at my mouth, and give them warning from me."* (Ezekiel 3:17)

2) PROPHETS ARE AGENTS OF RESTORATION

Remember, Elisha restored life to the shunammite woman's son.

And when Elisha was come into the house, behold, the child was dead, and laid upon his bed. He went in therefore, and shut the door upon them twain, and prayed unto the Lord. And he went up, and lay upon the child, and put his mouth upon his mouth, and his eyes upon his eyes, and his hands upon his hands: and stretched himself upon the child; and the flesh of the child waxed warm. Then he returned, and walked in the house to and fro; and went up, and stretched himself upon him: and the child sneezed seven times, and the child opened his eyes. And he called Gehazi, and said, Call this Shunammite. So he called her. And when she was come in unto him, he said, Take up thy son. Then she went in, and fell at his feet, and bowed herself to the ground, and took up her son, and went out.
2 Kings 4:32-37

And it came to pass after these things that the son of the woman, the mistress of the house, fell sick; and his sickness was so sore, that there was no breath left in him. And she said unto Elijah, What have I to do with thee, O thou man of God? art thou come unto me to call my sin to remembrance, and to slay my son? And he said unto her, Give me thy son. And he took him out of her bosom, and carried him up into a loft, where he abode, and laid him upon his own bed. And he cried unto the Lord, and said, O Lord my God, hast thou also brought evil upon the widow with whom I sojourn, by slaying her son? And he stretched himself upon the child three times, and cried unto the Lord, and said, O Lord my God, I pray thee, let this child's soul come into him again. And the Lord heard the voice of Elijah; and the soul of the child came into him again, and he revived. And Elijah took the child, and brought him down out of the chamber into the house, and delivered him unto his mother: and Elijah said, See, thy son liveth. And the woman said to Elijah, Now by this I know that thou art a man of God, and that the word of the Lord in thy mouth is truth.
1 Kings 17:17-24

PROPHETS ARE TOO MUCH TO WATCH AND TOO DANGEROUS TO MOCK

Talking about Jesus when he was born ("rabboni" meaning "the prophet of prophets"), the Bible says, *"Behold, this child is set for the fall and rising again of many in Israel; and for a sign which shall be spoken against."*

(Luke 2:34)

Recall how Elisha the prophet destroyed 42 children after they mocked him. *"And he went up from thence unto Bethel: and as he was going up by the way, there came forth little children out of the city, and mocked him, and said unto him, Go up, thou bald head; go up, thou bald head. And he turned back, and looked on them, and cursed them in the name of the Lord. And there came forth two she bears out of the wood, and tare forty and two children of them."* (2 Kings 2:23-24)

BE WARNED!

ALL GOD'S PROPHETS ARE TOO MUCH TO WATCH AND TOO DANGEROUS TO MOCK.

3) PROPHETS ARE AGENTS OF BLESSING & CURSES

Matthew tells me, *"He that receiveth a prophet in the name of a prophet shall receive a prophet's reward; and he that receiveth a righteous man in the name of a righteous man shall receive a righteous man's reward."* (Matthew 10:41)

GOD'S PROPHETS ARE AGENTS OF BLESSINGS & CURSES.

4) PROPHETS ARE AGENTS OF HEALING

Recall again how Elijah healed the son of the widow of zarephat at Zidon in first Kings. (1 Kings 17:17-24) Remember how Elisha healed the son of the shunammite woman in second Kings. "All God prophets are agents of HEALING." (2 Kings 4:32)

5) PROPHETS ARE AGENTS OF BREAKTHORUGH

In Ezra 4:24, the Bible recorded that the work of the house of the lord ceased. Until the prophet of God aroused the work of the house of God could not go forward.

Then the prophets, Haggai the prophet, and Zechariah the son of Iddo, prophesied unto the Jews that were in Judah and Jerusalem in the name of the God of Israel, even unto them. Then rose up Zerubbabel the son of Shealtiel, and Jeshua the son of Jozadak, and began to build the house of God which is at Jerusalem: and with them were the prophets of God helping them.
Ezra 5:2

We are bound to prosper when we believe in the Lord our God. *"Believe in the Lord your God, so shall ye be established; believe his prophets, so shall ye prosper."* (2 Chronicle 20:20)

6) PROPHETS ARE AGENTS OF DELIVERANCE

The prophet of God you receive and accept is the channel of your deliverance from God.

If there be a messenger with him, an interpreter, one among a thousand, to shew unto man his uprightness: Then he is gracious unto him, and saith, Deliver him from going down to the pit: I have found a ransom.
Job 3 3:23-24

Recall how Jesus (the prophet of prophets) found in the book of the prophet Esaias from the book of Luke. *"To preach deliverance to the captives, and recovering of sight to the blind, to set at liberty them that are bruised."* (Luke 4:18)

CONDITIONS TO HEAR FROM GOD

WALKING IN THE SPIRIT

But the natural man receiveth not the things of the Spirit of God: for they are foolishness unto him: neither can he know them, because they are spiritually discerned.
1 Corinthians 2:14

If we live in the Spirit, let us also walk in the Spirit.
Galatians 5:25

Every man/woman of the Spirit is a prophet/prophetess of God in the making. *"This I say then, Walk in the Spirit, and ye shall not fulfil the lust of the flesh."* (Galatians 5:16) We must walk in the SPIRIT to HEAR from GOD. *"I was in the Spirit on the Lord's day, and heard behind me a great voice, as of a trumpet."* (Revelation 1:10)

FAITH

In my opinion, it takes faith to hear from God. *"For unto whomsoever much is given, of him shall be much required: and to whom men have committed much, of him they will ask the more."* (Luke 12:48)

Everyone who really desires to hear from God must be a man/woman of faith. *"We having the same spirit of faith, according as it is written, I believed, and therefore have I spoken; we also believe, and therefore speak."* (2 Corinthians 4:13)

Remember...

But without faith it is impossible to please him: for he that cometh to God must believe that he is, and that he is a rewarder of them that diligently seek him.
Hebrews 11:6

WALK IN AGREEMENT

We must walk in agreement with Holy Spirit if we must hear from God. *"Again I say unto you, That if two of you shall agree on earth as touching anything that they shall ask, it shall be done for them of my Father which is in heaven."* (Matthew 18:19) *"Can two walk together, except they both agreed?"* (Amos 3:3)

WALK IN LOVE

God is our loving Father who takes pleasure to SPEAK to every one of us. We are admonished be the scripture to walk in love

Remember...

When Solomon walked in "love," God not only spoke to him but appeared to him. *"And Solomon loved the Lord, walking in the statutes of David his father: only he sacrificed and burnt incense in high places."* (1 Kings 3:3)

Every time we walk in love, the holy spirit appears and speaks to us. *"In Gibeon the Lord appeared to Solomon in a dream by night: and God said, Ask what I shall give thee."* (1 Kings 3:5)

I dare you to walk in love with God and witness the deep revelations the Holy Spirit will unfold unto you.

And we have known and believed the love that God hath to us. God is love; and he that dwelleth in love dwelleth in God, and God in him.
1 John 4:16

WALK IN TRUTH

Remember…

THE HOLY SPIRIT IS THE SPIRIT OF TRUTH

From my own prophetic office experience, every time we walk in truth, we prophesy accurately by the help of the Holy Ghost. *"I have heard what the prophets said, that prophesy lies in my name, saying, I have dreamed, I have dreamed. How long shall this be in the heart of the prophets that prophesy lies? yea, they are prophets of the deceit of their own heart."* (Jeremiah 23:25-26) *"Who is he that saith, and it cometh to pass, when the Lord commandeth it not?"* (Lamentations 3:37) Unless God says a thing in truth to you, you shall forever suffer punishment for walking in disobedience and lying spirits.

Howbeit when he, the Spirit of truth, is come, he will guide you into all truth: for he shall not speak of himself; but whatsoever he shall hear, that shall he speak: and he will shew you things to come.
John 16:13

If we say that we have no sin, we deceive ourselves, and the truth is not in us. If we confess our sins, he is faithful and just to forgive us our sins, and to cleanse us from all unrighteousness. If we say that we have not sinned, we make him a liar, and his word is not in us.
1 John 1:8-10

WHAT IS SIN?

Every time you willingly or involuntarily disobey the word of God, you have sinned. Every time you go contrary to the scriptures by committing immorality of any kind, you have sinned. Every time you falsely accuse others, gossip against others, disobey the 10 commandments—you have sinned. Everytime you hate others for no just reason, you have sinned. We must immitate Jesus and show love to all around us.

Remember...

Jesus said unto him, Thou shalt love the Lord thy God with all thy heart, and with all thy soul, and with all thy mind. This is the first and great commandment. And the second is like unto it, Thou shalt love thy neighbour as thyself.
Matthew 22:37-39

The pleasure of sin is exciting, but it is for a season. The lifestyle of sin is pleasurable, but it is short-lived. Just like the Bible attested in the book of Proverbs, *"But the end thereof are the ways of death."* (Proverbs 16:25) The end result of a sinful man is full of calamity and destruction.

Recall again with me, *"But she that liveth in pleasure is dead while she liveth."* (1 Timothy 5:8)

Remember, *"The pleasure of sin is but for a season."* (Hebrews 11:25) Recall what was said of Moses: *"Choosing rather to suffer affliction with the people of God, than to enjoy the pleasures of sin for a season."* (Hebrews 11:25)

Although one man said SIN is short for "**Sa**tan **I**dentification **N**umber," it is not incorrect but it is incomplete. In my own definition, sin is disobeying God's words and commandments. Every time you operate outside of the commandment of God, you are committing sin. *"He that committeth sin is of the devil; for the devil sinneth from the beginning. For this purpose the son of God was manifested that he might destroy the works of the devil."* (1 John 3:8)

He that covereth his sins shall not prosper: but whoso confesseth and forsaketh them shall have mercy.
Proverbs 28:13

Be not overcome of evil, but overcome evil with good.
Romans 12:21

We must stop any form of oppression to others and the lifestyle of wickedness. It is written, *"Oh let the wickedness of the wicked come to an end; but establish the just: for the righteous God trieth the hearts and reins."* (Psalms 7:9)

Remember…

The evil bow before the good; and the wicked at the gates of the righteous.
Proverbs 14:19

ACKNOWLEGDE THAT YOU ARE A SINNER

Although David said in Psalms 51:3, *"For I acknowledge my transgressions and my sin is ever before me,"* we must fight sin with all our heart. *"For sin shall not have dominion over you: for ye are not under the law, but under grace."* (Romans 6:14)

WHO IS A SINNER?

Know ye not, that to whom ye yield yourselves servants to obey, his servants ye are to whom ye obey; whether of sin unto death, or of obedience unto righteousness?
Romans 6:16

As long as we yield to sin, we shall remain captive and prey to the enemy.

Examine yourselves, whether ye be in the faith; prove your own selves. Know ye not your own selves, how that Jesus Christ is in you, except ye be reprobates?
2 Corinthians 13:5

Although most faith people live in denial about the work of the flesh, from my own scriptural understanding, everyone operating within the scope of Galatians 5:20-21 is classified as a sinner.

Now the works of the flesh are manifest, which are these; Adultery, fornication, uncleanness, lasciviousness, idolatry, witchcraft, hatred, variance, emulations, wrath, strife, seditions, heresies, envyings, murders, drunkenness, revellings, and such like: of the which I tell you before, as I have also told you in time past, that they which do such things shall not inherit the kingdom of God.
Galatians 5:20-21

Further supporting scripture...

But the fearful, and unbelieving, and the abominable, and murderers, and whoremongers, and sorcerers, and idolaters, and all liars, shall have their part in the lake which burneth with fire and brimstone: which is the second death.
Revelation 21:8

WHO, THEREFORE, IS A SINNER?

1) The Lazy Man: It is sinful for any able body man/woman to fold their hand and make themselves beggars. The Bible says, *"the sluggard will not plow by reason of the cold; therefore shall he beg in harvest, and have nothing."* (Proverbs 20:4) In my understanding, laziness is a sin. *"For even when we were with you, this we commanded you, that if any would not work, neither should he eat."* (2 Thessalonians 3:10) \

Covenant mentality demands that we all understand that God has done His part over our lives. Jesus said I must work. It is dignified for every believer to earn money through the work of their hands.

Although most lazy people live in denial and tend to blame someone else, nevertheless, Godliness demands that we take absolute responsibility for the outcome of our lives.

2) Unbelievers: In my view, all that have not acknowledged Jesus Christ as Lord and savior are sinners. The Bible says *God heareth not sinners*. Without contradiction, all unbelievers live in a sinful lifestyle. Unless God has mercy, most unbelievers will not make eternity in heaven.

3) Liars: *"All liars, shall have their part in the lake which burneth with fire and brimstone: which is the second death."* (Revelation 21:8) Someone whom I know very well lies so much to themselves, they became a beggar by paralyzing their future and frustrating the will of God over their life.

HOW DO I COME OUT OF SIN?

You must REPENT, CONFESS and PROCLAIM the LORD JESUS CHRIST. The word says as many as received him, to them gave He power to become the sons of God. Even to them that believe on his name.

To qualify for divine visitation, do the following (with sincerity):

1) *Acknowledge* that you are a sinner and that He died for you. (Romans 3:23)

2) *Repent of your sins.* (Acts 3:19, Luke 13:5, 2 Peter 3:9)

3) *Believe in your heart* that Jesus died for your sin. (Romans 10:10)

4) *Confess Jesus as the Lord over your life.* (Romans 10:10, Acts 2:21)

Now repeat this Prayer after me—

Say Lord Jesus, I accept you today, as my Lord and my savior, forgive me of my sins wash me with your blood. Right now, I believe, I am sanctified, I am save, I am free, I am free from the Power of sin to serve the Lord Jesus. Thank you Lord for saving me. Amen.

Congratulations.

YOU ARE NOW A BORN AGAIN CHRISTIAN!

STEPS TO OVERCOME THE LIFESTYLE OF SIN

FAITH

*But without faith it is impossible to please him:
for he that cometh to God must believe that he is,
and that he is a rewarder of them
that diligently seek him.*
Hebrews 11:6

It takes faith to make solid decision concerning the lifestyle of sin. "Yea, a man may say, Thou hast faith, and I have works: shew me thy faith without thy works, and I will shew thee my faith by my works." (James 2:18)

DECISION

Unless we make up our mind, sin has the power to dominate us. Decisions are the wheels of destiny—we either ride into shame or fame.

For sin shall not have dominion over you: for ye are not under the law, but under grace.
Romans 6:14

PRAYER

Prayer alone sets the standard for the lifestyle

of sin to stop. It is written, *"Watch and pray, that ye enter not into temptation: the spirit indeed is willing, but the flesh is weak."* (Matthew 26:41)

HOW TO ACTIVATE THE HOLY SPIRIT IN YOUR LIFE

First of all, you must believe that there is a Holy Spirit.

1) ***Acknowledge*** the person of the Holy Spirt.

2) ***Believe*** in the ministration of the Holy Spirit.

3) ***Submit & obey*** the person of the Holy Spirit.

4) ***Welcome*** the sweet presence of the Holy Spirit.

SUMMARY OF CHAPTER ONE

—Prophets of God are agents of God's solution for man's situation.

—Prophets are agents of solution for all our frustrations.

—Prophets are agents of restoration.

—Prophets are agents of healing.

—Prophets are agents of breakthrough.

—Prophets are agents of blessings and curses.

—Prophets are too much to watch, but too dangerous to mock.

—*"Surely the Lord God will do nothing, but he revealeth his secret unto his servants the prophets."* (AMOS 3:7)

CHAPTER 2

THE MYSTERY OF THE PROPHETIC WORD

Knowing this first, that no prophecy of the scripture is of any private interpretation.
2 Peter 1:20

The prophetic ministry comes with mysteries that cannot be understood in the energy of the flesh. As long as you are operating in the physical, you will miss the doings of the Lord in the prophetic ministry. *"Heaven and earth shall pass away: but my words shall not pass away."* (Luke 21:33)

Unless God has not spoken to you, but if the LORD has spoken a word to you, take it from me—it is only a question of time. *"For I am the Lord: I will speak, and the word that I shall speak shall come to pass; it shall be no more prolonged: for in your days, O rebellious house, will I say the word, and will perform it, saith the Lord God."* (Ezekiel 12:25)

Therefore say unto them, Thus saith the Lord God; There shall none of my words be prolonged any more, but the word which I have spoken shall be done, saith the Lord God.
Ezekiel 12:28

The prophetic ministry is no cheap talk. It takes a man of the spirit to understand the doings of the Lord. *"But the natural man receiveth not the things of the Spirit of God: for they are foolishness unto him: neither can he know them, because they are spiritually discerned."* (1 Corinthians 2:14)

It is God that calls any man. *"Before I formed thee in the belly I knew thee; and before thou camest forth out of the womb I sanctified thee, and I ordained thee a prophet unto the nations."* (Jeremiah 1:5) Although God calls all of us, we must carry these attributes to genuinely operate in the prophetic mysteries.

THE MERIT FOR THE OFFICE OF A PROPHET

MEEKNESS

The meek will he guide in judgment: and the meek will he teach his way.
Pslams 25:9

But the fruit of the Spirit is love, joy, peace, longsuffering, gentleness, goodness, faith, Meekness, temperance: against such there is no law. And they that are Christ's have crucified the flesh with the affections and lusts.
Galatians 5:22-24

*If there be a messenger with him, an interpreter,
one among a thousand, to shew unto man
his uprightness.*
Job 33:23

*And he gave some, apostles; and some, prophets;
and some, evangelists; and some, pastors and teachers.*
Ephesians 4:11

Despite our area of calling God speaks to everyone. God speaks to the Apostle, the prophet, the evangelist, the pastor and the teacher. Even the laitys and all the clergymen and the bishops are all called by God. The Bible says many are called, but few are chosen. To tell you the truth, God speaks to you even daily. The good news about the mystery of the prophetic ministry is that God can speak to anyone from their own dream, vision and revelation.

Let's briefly examine dreams, vision and revelation.

OUR DREAMS

GOD USES OUR DREAM TO WARN US

It is written, *"For God speaketh once, yea twice, yet man perceiveth it not. In a dream, in a vision of the night, when deep sleep falleth upon men, in slumberings upon the bed."* (Job 33:14-15)

God uses our dreams to warn us and to reveal

to us things to come. For example, God warned Abimelech concerning Abraham's wife Sarah, whom he took. *"But God came to Abimelech in a dream by night, and said to him, Behold, thou art but a dead man, for the woman which thou hast taken; for she is a man's wife."* (Genesis 20:3)

God warned Pontus Pilate through his wife dream about the unrighteous judgement against Jesus Christ. *"Have thou nothing to do with that just man: for I have suffered many things this day in a dream because of him."* (Matthew 27:19)

VISION

GOD USES VISION TO SHOW US GRAPHIC PICTURES OF OUR FUTURE & DESTINIES

For the vision is yet for an appointed time, but at the end it shall speak, and not lie: though it tarry, wait for it; because it will surely come, it will not tarry.
Habakkuk 2:3

Concerning Abram, *"After these things the word of the Lord came unto Abram in a vision, saying, Fear not, Abram: I am thy shield, and thy exceeding great reward."* (Genesis 15:1)

*And it shall come to pass afterward, that I will
pour out my spirit upon all flesh; and your
sons and your daughters shall prophesy,
your old men shall dream dreams,
your young men shall see visions.*
Joel 2:28

Concerning Moses, *"And he said, Hear now my words: If there be a prophet among you, I the Lord will make myself known unto him in a vision, and will speak unto him in a dream."* (Numbers 12:6)

REVELATION

GOD USES REVELATION TO REVEAL HIS AGENDA CONCERNING US

Concerning Jesus, God revealed to John, *"The Revelation of Jesus Christ, which God gave unto him, to shew unto his servants things which must shortly come to pass; and he sent and signified it by his angel unto his servant John."* (Revelation 1:1)

CHAPTER 3
ENGAGING THE PROPHETIC WORD

This charge I commit unto thee, son Timothy, according to the prophecies which went before on thee, that thou by them mightest war a good warfare.
1 Timothy 1:18

With the accreditation as a spiritual law enforcement official with a warrant for the arrest of the devil, we must all enforce the prophetic word concerning our destines.

Before I formed thee in the belly I knew thee; and before thou camest forth out of the womb I sanctified thee, and I ordained thee a prophet unto the nations
Jeremiah 1:5

WE ARE ALL CALLED BY GOD

It is written, *"For many are called, but few are chosen."* (Matthew 22:14)

WE MUST WALK IN THE AREA OF OUR CALLING IN LIFE

*For I would that all men were even as I myself.
But every man hath his proper gift of God,
one after this manner, and another after that.*
1 Corinthians 7:7

WE MUST STAY IN THE AREA OF OUR CALLING IN LIFE

*But as God hath distributed to every man,
as the Lord hath called every one, so let him walk.
And so ordain I in all churches.*
1 Corinthians 7:17

*Let every man abide in the same calling
wherein he was called.*
1 Corinthians 7:20

*Brethren, let every man, wherein he is called,
therein abide with God.*
1 Corinthians 7:24

We must therefore pursue our God ordained prophetic word for our lives. *"A man's gift maketh room for him, and bringeth him before great men."* (Proverbs 18:16)

PRAYER POINTS TO ENFORCE OUR PROPHETIC WORD

1. Father Lord, by the power in the Blood of Jesus, and by the help of the Holy Ghost, scatter and destroy any hindering spirit around me, in the name of Jesus.

2. Father Lord, scatter and destroy the power of devouring spirit and limitation, in the name of Jesus.

3. Father Lord, any decree made upon my feet because I have come to Christ, let it be revoked in Jesus name.

4. Father Lord, let my feet be anointed and washed by your blood to lead me to peaceful places, in the name of Jesus.

5. Father Lord, release the spirit of carpenter upon me to destroy the horns of enemies, in the name of Jesus.

6. Any decree to cause satanic road-block in my way of breakthrough, be scattered by fire, in the name of Jesus.

7. Father Lord, come and be our shepherd, to keep us together and save us from thieves, in Jesus name.

8. Every satanic or collective power that wants to scatter what I have gathered, I command you to fall down and die, in the name of Jesus.

9. Association of evil, gang-up on witchcraft power to cause derailment in my life and scatter by fire, in the name of Jesus.

10. Any power put in place to supervise and confirm failure in my life, die by fire, in the name of Jesus.

11. Anything in me contradicting the word of God to cause error, die by fire, in the name of Jesus.

12. Any power making a decree to affect my standing in the Lord, break by fire, in the name of Jesus.

13. Evil decree or curse over my life, spiritually, physically, financially, matrimonially and educationally, I break you, in the name of Jesus.

14. Anything in me, around me, within me, contesting with the presence of Holy Spirit in me, are you still alive? Die forever and perish, in the name of Jesus.

15. Spirit of the Living God, arise and take me to my place of blessing now, in Jesus name.

16. Father Lord, whatever weapon or tricks of the enemy to steal, kill and destroy, destroy them with their weapon forever, in Jesus name.

17. Father Lord, connect, correct and direct my helpers to me everywhere—anywhere they may be—in the

name of Jesus.

18. Spirit of the living God, arise and remove any evil veil covering my face so I can see, in Jesus name.

19. Power to succeed in life, come upon me now, in the name of Jesus.

20. Power to see and discern, come upon me, in the name of Jesus.

21. Power to overcome, fall upon me now, in the name of Jesus.

DECISION KEYS

1) Nothing changes until you make up your mind.

2) Decision is the gateway to deliverance.

3) Until you decide, no one will decide for you.

4) Your prosperity is proportional to your decisions.

5) The decision you make will determine the future you will create

6) Decision creates future and fulfills destinies.

7) Decision beautifies our future.

8) Decision keeps you out of trouble.

9) Decision exempts you from evil.

10) Decision gurantees eternity.

11) You can only go far in life by your faith decisions.

12) You are poor because you made such decisions

13) Make a decision and change your life.

14) Life changing decisions are a function of quality

information.

15) Success in life is a function of decision.

16) Life experiences are full of decisions.

17) Decisions change destinies.

18) Never settle for information—always look for revelation.

19) You are where you are today based on your last decision.

20) Information is crucial in decision making.

21) Decision makers rule the world.

22) You can rule your world with quality decisions.

23) As long as you decide rightly, Satan cannot harrass you.

HEALING KEYS

1) Always carry a positive mindset, regardless of the prevailing circumstances.

2) Always tell yourself the truth before you lie about it.

3) If the truth be told, you are a branch of His blessings, the planting of the Lord.

4) Never confess that you are sick to the hearing of the member of your body.

5) Positive confession with faith yields positive results.

6) Every cures of man have no power to prevail over your life.

7) A merry heart is medicinal and health to your body.

8) Spiritual and emotional well-being is vital to happiness in life.

9) To avoid depression, never have regrets.

10) Never be anxious in life to avoid anxiety.

11) Always live today for today to be at peace with your spirit and with God.

12) You're unique because your challenges are tailored to you only.

13) The blessing always dominates the curses any day.

14) Decisions are the wheels of life.

15) We either ride into fame or into shame.

16) Daily exercise and some reading of the Bible gurantees good health.

17) Every day is God's day. No day created by God is a disapointment.

18) Stay away from sweet stuff—they are temporary.

19) Sugar is sweet to your taste, beware! It also contributes to diabetes.

20) A good prayer life gurantees longivity.

21) People that pray in tongues do not develop mental disease.

22) Always be positive in everything.

23) Always have a mentor in life that will oppose and fight the tormentor.

24) Always have someone in life to learn from.

25) Tell everybody what you plan to do and someone will help you do it.

26) Winners fight to the last.

27) Quitters never win in life.

28) Soul winners are heirs to the kingdom of god.

29) Soul winners never lack help.

30) Soul winners are cerified with divine help.

31) God is always looking for soul winners to bless.

32) Life is a warfare and not a funfare.

33) In life you fight for all you possess.

34) No man or woman was born rich.

35) In your lifetime do something positive to impact your world.

36) Take care of your life today—you don't have one to spare.

37) Take your life serious before the devil take you down.

38) Always be cheerful at all times.

39) Regardless of the prevailing circumstances around

you, your life is in the hand of God.

40) God is the super surgeon that will spiritually-surgically heal you.

41) Always expect help from above and not from abroad.

42) Man will disappoint you, but god will appoint you.

43) The joy of the lord is always our strength.

44) Spiritual height is not measured in length or breath.

45) If you go deeper with God, you will see deeper.

46) Your next level in life is full of recognition.

47) Go to where you are celebrated and not where you are tolerated.

48) Develop yourself in the area of your calling in life.

49) A lifestyle of thanks given keeps God 24/7 on duty on our behalf.

50) Develop a lifestyle of thanksgiving.

51) Thanksgiving guarantees our access to obtain the promises.

PRAYER POINTS FOR THE HELP OF THE HOLY SPIRIT

1) Father Lord, deliver me from this present trial, in the name of Jesus.

2) Almighty Father, bring me out of this present obscurity, in the name of Jesus.

3) Holy Spirit, help me to overcome this trial, in Jesus name.

4) Holy Spirit, speak to me, in the name of Jesus.

5) Holy Spirit, minister to my subconscious spirit, in the name of Jesus.

6) Fire of God, burn down every mountain of difficulty, in the name of Jesus.

7) Holy Ghost, baptize me with your fire, in the name of Jesus.

8) Holy Spirit, go before me and favor me in this present challenge, in the name of Jesus.

9) Spirit of God, grant me liberty and freedom by the fire of the Holy Spirit, in the name of Jesus.

10) Father Lord, intervene on my behalf, in the name

of Jesus.

11) Ancient of day, liberate me this season, in the name of Jesus.

12) Immortal redeemer, bring me higher above these prevailing changes.

13) Lord God, turn this present obstacale into my miracle, in the name of Jesus.

14) Fire of God, break down these obstacles for me, in the name of Jesus.

15) Holy Spirit, favor me in, Jesus name.

16) Holy Spirit. release me from this challenge, in the name of Jesus.

17) Holy Spirit, become my compionion, in Jesus name.

18) Holy Spirit, represent me in this matter.

19) Holy Spirit, elevant me beyond my own immagination, in the name of Jesus.

20) Holy Spirit, do not allow my enemies to truimph over my life, in the name of Jesus.

21) Fire of God, protect me, in the name of Jesus.

22) Fire of God, destroy my enemies, in the name of Jesus.

23) Fire of God, build a wall around me, in the name of Jesus.

24) Fire of God, expose my enemies, in the name of Jesus.

25) Fire of God, prove yourself, in the name of Jesus.

26) Holy Spirit, represent me in jesus name.

27) Holy Spirit, release your boldnes into my life.

28) Holy Spirit, grant me signs and wonders.

29) Holy Spirit, make me a living wonder in my lifetime.

30) Holy Spirit, turn my life around, in the name of Jesus.

31) Holy Spirit, I will not remain at this level, in the name of Jesus.

32) Spirit of God, lift me higher, in the mighty name of Jesus.

33) Angels of God, minister unto me, in the name of Jesus.

34) Hand of God, separate me this season, in the name of Jesus.

CONCLUSION

Despise not prophesyings.
1 Thessalonians 5:20

The prophetic ministry is a noble ministry that operates on a higher standard. The prophetic ministry demands high level of self discipline. It is written, *"For unto whomsoever much is given, of him shall be much required: and to whom men have committed much, of him they will ask the more."* (Luke 12:48)

IN THE PROPHETIC MINISTRY WE MUST ALL DEPEND HEAVILY ON THE HOLY SPIRIT

WE MUST ALL DEVELOP A STRONG BOND AND RELATIONSHIP WITH THE PERSON OF THE HOLY SPIRIT

I believe it is time to begin a relationship with the Holy Spirit. Always practice to welcome the Holy Spirit every morning and every day of your life. Learn to pray often.

Let us hear the conclusion of the whole matter:
Fear God, and keep his commandments:
for this is the whole duty of man.
For God shall bring every work into judgment, with every secret thing, whether it be good, or whether it be evil.
Ecclesiastes 12:13-14

This book will end just like any other storybook, unless we make a genuine commitment to seek the face of the Lord. It is written, *"For God shall bring every work into judgment, with every secret thing, whether it be good, or whether it be evil."* (Ecclesiastes 12:14) If you are a born again Christian, we'd like to encourage you in your Christian life. If you are not a born again Christian, we can help you here receive genuine salvation.

Therefore if any man be in Christ, he is a new creature:
old things are passed away;
behold, all things are become new.
2 Corinthians 5:17

Now repeat this prayer after me:

Say Lord Jesus, I accept you today, as my Lord and my savior. Forgive me of my sins, wash me with your blood. Right now, I believe I am sanctified, I am saved, I am free. I am free from the power of sin, to serve the Lord Jesus. Thank you Lord for saving me. Amen.

Congratulations. You are now...

...a BORN AGAIN CHRISTIAN.

Again I say to you—CONGRATULATIONS!

What must I do to determine genuine salvation?

To determine divine visitation you must be

born again! The word says as many as received him, to them gave He power to become the sons of God. Even to them that believe on his name.

To qualify for SALVATION, do the following sincerely:

1) Acknowledge that you are a sinner and that He died for you. (Romans 3:23)

2) Repent of your sins. (Acts 3:19, Luke 13:5, 2 Peter 3:9)

3) Believe in your heart that Jesus died for your sin. (Romans 10:10)

4) Confess Jesus as the Lord over your life. (Romans 10:10, Acts 2:21)

NOW REPEAT THIS PRAYER AFTER ME:
Say Lord Jesus, I accept you today, as my Lord and my savior, forgive me of my sins wash me with your blood. Right now, I believe, I am sanctified, I am save, I am free, I am free from the Power of sin to serve the Lord Jesus. Thank you Lord for saving me. Amen.

Congratulations.

YOU ARE NOW A BORN AGAIN CHRISTAIN!

Again, I say to you—congratulations!

I adjure you to watch the Spirit of God bear witness with your Spirit confirming His word with signs following. The word says the Spirit itself beareth witness with our spirit, that we are the children of God. Join a bible believing church or join us on our weekly and Sunday worship services at 343 Sanford Avenue Newark New Jersey 07106.

Chapter 3 Engaging the Prophetic Word

WISDOM KEYS

— Every productive society is a society heading to the top.

—Millions of Nigerians run away from Nigeria. Very few Nigerians stay in Nigeria.

—My decision to return Nigeria is the will of God for my life.

—My shortcoming in America after 18 years is the fact that I've trained me to be wise, to think, reflect and reason appropriately.

—If you train your mind to reason, it will train your hands to earn money.

—It is absurd to use the money of the heathen to build the kingdom of the living God.

—Every ministry reveals its agenda and VISION either at the beginning or at the end.

—Be careful of your life. It is your first ministry.

—The average American mind is conditioned for a continual quest to get new things and discard the old.

—When I considered well, my BMW jeep became my initial deposit for the work of the ministry in Nigeria.

—Money will never fall from any tree or person. Make up your mind to be independent today.

—Everyone is waiting for you to change your mind. Until you change your thinking, nothing changes around you.

—Multiple academic degrees in other disciplines gave me the chance to think and reason.

—Whatever anyone is thinking at any time reveals what is inside of their heart.

—All planned events are the product of meditation.

—Every event is designed for a designated timeline.

—Wisdom is your ability to think, to create and invent.

— If you can think wisely enough, you will come out of debt.

—The distance between you and your success is your innovative and creative ability to think well.

—Success is the result of hard work, commitment, resolve and determined learning from past mistakes and failings.

—If you organize your mind, you have organized your life and destiny.

—There is a thin line between success and failure.

—Wealth is your ability to think, power is your ability to reason and success is your ability to be informed.

—If you can make use of your mind by thinking and reasoning, God will make use of your life and destiny.

—Reflect, reason, think and be Great.

—Famous people are born of woman.

—That you will make it is your intention, that you will survive is your resolve, that you will succeed with changes is your determination, personal efforts and hard work.

—No man was born a failure.

—Lack of vision is the result of failure.

—Working with mental patients encourages and aspire me to be a productive observant and dedicated to my assignment.

—Successful people are not magicians. It is the will-power, combined with hard work and determination and a resolve to succeed, that make them succeed.

—In the unequivocal state of the mind, intention is not a location or a position. It is the state of the mind.

—So many people think that they think.

—The mind is used to think, to reflect and to reason.

—You will remain blind with your eyes open until you can see with your mind by thinking.

—There is no favoritism in accurate and precise calculation.

—Although knowledge is power, information is the key and gateway to a great future.

—It will take the hand of God to move the hand of man.

—With the backing of the great wise God, nothing will disconnect you from your inheritance.

—As long as you have wisdom and understanding of God, Satan and evil cannot manipulate your life and destiny.

—You have come this far in life by your own judgment and the decisions you made in the past. Now lean in and listen to God for another dimension of greatness.

—Great people are ordinary people. It is extra ordinary efforts and the price of sacrifice that produces greatness in them.

—As a mental direct care worker, I saw a great pastor and a motivational speaker within myself.

—A menial job does not reduce your self-worth. Until you resolve to achieve greatness and see greatness in all you do, you will never count in your community.

—The principle of Jesus will solve your gambling and addiction problems.

—The man of Jesus will lead you into heaven.

—Everyone has their self-appraisal and what they think about you. Until you discover yourself, other opinions about you will alter the real you.

—Supervisors and directors are just a position in the chain of command in a workplace. Never allow your supervisor hierarchy to alter your opinion of yourself.

—Everyone can come out of debt if they make up their mind.

—The fact that I am not a decision-maker at work does

not diminish my contribution to my world.

—Although it appears like it was a poor decision to accept a direct care employment at a psychiatric hospital, as I reflect on my nine years of that experience, it became apparent that I have learned and experienced enough for my next assignment.

—Self-encouragement and determination is a resolve of the heart.

—If you are determined to make a difference and do the things that make a difference, you will eventually make a difference.

—Good things do not come easy.

—Short cuts will cut your life short.

—Those who look ahead move ahead.

—Life is all about making an impact. In your lifetime strive to make an impact in your community.

—Make friends and connect with people who are moving ahead of you in life.

—If you can look around well, you have come a long way in your life, made a lot of difference and realized a lot of success in life.

—If you are my old friend, hurry up to reach out to me before I become a stranger to you.

—I am blessed with inspirations from God that changed my interpretation of the world around me.

—I thought I was stagnant and lonely until I looked around and noticed my children running around and my wife cooking.

— At 40, I resigned my job to seek the Lord forever.

—My ministry took a drastic rise to the top when the wisdom of God visited me with knowledge and understanding.

—You will be a better person if you understand the characteristics of your personality like your mood swings, attitudes and habits.

—It is the seed of love you sow into the heart of a child and a woman that you reap in due time.

—Love is not selfish. Love shares everything, including the concealed secrets of the mind.

—As long as you have a prayer life and a Bible, you will never feel lonely in the race of life.

—When good friends disconnect from you, let them

go. They might have seen something new in a different direction.

—Confidence in yourself and in God is the only way to bring you out of captivity

—Never train a child to waste his or her time.

—The mind is the greatest asset of a great future.

—You walk by common sense, run by principles and fly by instruction.

—Those who become successful in life did it by self-determination, hard work and learning from past failures.

—Most successful people are lonely people. No one renders help to them, believing they are already successful. Except when they seek for more knowledge and information, they are all alone.

— I have seen a towing truck vehicle. I have also seen a towing ship in the water. But I have never seen a towing airplane in the air.

—I exercise my judgment and make a decision every minute of the day. Decisions are crucial, critical and vital with reference to your future.

—So many people wish for a great future. You can

only work towards a great future.

—Your celebrity status began when you discovered your talent. What are you good at? Work at it with all your commitment.

—Prayers will sustain you, but the wisdom of God will prosper you.

—When I met Oyedepo, his teachings changed my perspective. But when I met Ibiyeomie, his teachings changed my perception.

— I will be successful in ministry if only I concentrate and focus my energy in the work of the ministry.

— It took the late Dr. Norman Vincent Peale's book to open my mind towards the kingdom of success.

CHAPTER 4
PRAYER OF SALVATION

I am glad you have read this book all the way from the beginning to this point. All I have said from the beginning will remain a mystery until you commit it into practice.

And before you do so, I want you—if you have not given your life to Jesus already—to do so now. Give your life to Christ. I want you to know the truth! The truth is that Jesus died for your sins and because He died, you must be alive and prosperous.

What must I do to determine my divine visitation?

To determine divine visitation, you must be born again! The word says, *"As many as received Him, to them gave He power to become the sons of God. Even to them that believe on his name."* (John 1:12)

To qualify for divine visitation, do the following with sincerity—

1) Acknowledge that you are a sinner and that He died for you. (Romans 3:23)
2) Repent of your sins. (Acts 3:19, Luke 13:5, 2 Peter 3:9)
3) Believe in your heart that Jesus died for your sins. (Romans 10:10)

4) Confess Jesus as the Lord over your life.
   (Romans 10:10, Acts 2:21)

Now repeat this prayer after me:

Say Lord Jesus, I accept you today, as my Lord and my savior. Forgive me of my sins, wash me with your blood. Right now, I believe I am sanctified, I am saved, I am free. I am free from the power of sin, to serve the Lord Jesus. Thank you Lord for saving me. Amen.

Congratulations. You are now...

A BORN AGAIN CHRISTIAN.

Again I say to you—CONGRATULATIONS!

I adjure you to watch the Spirit of God bear witness with your Spirit, confirming His word with subsequent signs. The word says, *"The Spirit itself beareth witness with our spirit, that we are the children of God."* (Romans 8:16)

MIRACLE CARE OUTREACH

*"...But that the members should have
the same care one for another"*
1 Corinthians 12:25

We are all members of the body of Christ. Jesus commanded us to love our neighbor as ourselves. This includes caring for one another as a member of one body. True love is expressed in caring and giving. The word says, for God so Love He gave....

Reach out to someone in need of Jesus. Help someone in crisis find Christ. Look out and prove your love to Jesus by caring and inviting your friends and associates to find Jesus the Healer.

Invite your friends to our Home Care Cell Fellowship (Miracle Chapel Intl. Satellite Fellowship). We're in the U.S. at 33 Schley Street, Newark, New Jersey 07112. Home Care Cell Fellowship Group meets every Tuesday at 6:00pm-7:00pm.

If you are in Nigeria—MIRACLE OF GOD MINISTRIES, aka "MIRACLE CHAPEL INTL." Mpama–Egbu-Owerri Imo state Nigeria.

LIFE IS NOT ALL ABOUT DURATION, BUT IT'S ALL ABOUT DONATION

What does this statement mean?
Life consists not in accumulation of material

wealth. (Luke 12:15) But it's all about liberality…i.e., what you can give and share with others. (Proverbs 11:25) When you live for others, you live forever—because you outlive your generation by the legacy you leave behind after you depart into glory to be with the Lord. But when you live for yourself, when you are reduced to SELF—you are easily forgotten when you die and depart in glory.

Permit me to admonish you today to live your life to be a blessing to a soul connected to you today. I want you to know that so many souls are connected and looking up to you, and through you so many souls will be saved and rescued from destruction. Will you disciple someone today to find Jesus Christ?

As a genuine Christian, it is your duty to evangelize Jesus Christ to all you meet on your way. Jesus is still in the healing business—Jesus is still doing miracles, from time of old to now. Therefore, tell someone about Jesus Christ today, disciple and bring them to Church. *Philip findeth Nathanael...* (John 1:45)

Please prove the sincerity of your love for God today, please become a soul winner. The dignity of your Christianity is hidden in your boldness to proclaim and evangelize Jesus Christ to all you meet on your way. There is a question mark on the integrity of your Christianity until you become a life soul winner. Invite someone to join us worship the Lord Jesus this coming Sunday. Amen.

MIRACLE OF GOD MINISTRIES
PILLARS OF THE COMMISSION

We Believe, Preach and Practice the following:

1) We believe and preach Salvation to every living human being.

2) We believe and preach Repentance and Forgiveness of sins.

3) We believe and preach the baptism of the Holy Spirit and Spiritual gifts.

4) We believe and teach Prosperity.

5) We believe and preach Divine Healing and Miracles—Signs and Wonder.

6) We believe and preach Faith.

7) We believe and proclaim the Power of God (Supernatural).

8) We believe and proclaim Praise and Worship to God.

9) We believe and preach Wisdom.

10) We believe and preach Holiness (Consecration).

11) We believe and preach Vision.

12) We believe and teach the Word of God.

13) We believe and teach Success.

14) We believe and practice Prayer.

15) We believe and teach Deliverance.

These 15 stones form the Pillars of Our Commission. Become part of this church family and follow this great move of God.

MY HEARTFELT PRAYER FOR YOU

It is my burning desire for God to touch you through one of our teaching books or CDs. It also my personal desire for you encounter God for yourself.

Now let me Pray for you:

I plead the precious blood of Jesus over your life. I decree and declare that no weapon fashioned against you shall ever prosper, every tongue that shall rise up against you God shall condemn it in judgement. From this day I declare your name in the lamb book of life. From this great day I declare goodness and mercy to hunt you down all the days of your life. Remain blessed, in Jesus name. Amen.

TIME TO TURN TO GOD

HAVE YOU EVER ASK WHY ARE YOU HERE? GOD PLANTED YOU HERE TO BRING TO PASS PLAN OVER YOUR LIFE

THE BEST OF YOUR PHYSICAL STRENGTH & EFFORTS IS THE START OF GOD'S GRACE

ETERNITY IS REAL. HEAVEN IS SURE. HELL IS INEVITABLE!!!

If you want to hear from God, you must repent and give your life to Jesus Christ.

Join us and worship the Lord Jesus Christ. We worship every Sunday morning from 10:00-12:00 at our miracle worship service. And every Wednesday night from 7:00-9:00pm, we have our Bible study/healing communion.

ABOUT THE AUTHOR

Rev. Franklin N. Abazie is the founding and Presiding Pastor of Miracle of God Ministries, with headquarters in Newark, New Jersey USA and a branch church in Owerri-Imo State Nigeria. He is following the footsteps of one of his mentors, the healing evangelist Oral Roberts of the blessed memory. The Lord passed Oral Roberts' healing mantle two days before he went to be with the Lord at age 91 into the hands of healing evangelist Rev. Franklin N. Abazie in a vision.

In all his services, the Power and Presence of God is present to heal all in his audience. Rev. Abazie is an ordained man of God, with a Healing Ministry reviving the healing and miracle ministry of Jesus Christ of Nazareth.

Pastor Franklin N. Abazie, has been called by God with a unique mandate: **"THE MOMENT IS DUE TO IMPACT YOUR WORLD THROUGH THE REVIVAL OF THE HEALING AND MIRACLE MINISTRY OF JESUS CHRIST OF NAZARETH.**

"I AM SENDING YOU TO RESTORE HEALTH UNTO THEE AND I WILL HEAL THEE OF THY WOUNDS, SAID THE LORD OF HOST."

Rev. Abazie is a gifted, ardent teacher of the word of God, who operates also in the office of a Prophet, generating and attracting undeniable signs and wonders, special miracles and healings, with apostolic fireworks of the Holy Ghost. He is the founding and presiding senior Pastor of this fast growing Healing Ministry. He has written over 86 inspirational, healing and transforming books covering almost all aspects of divine healing and life. He is happily married and blessed with children.

BOOKS BY REV. FRANKLIN N. ABAZIE:

1) The Outcome of Faith
2) Understanding the Secret of Prevailing Prayers
3) Commanding Abundance
4) Understanding the Secret of the Man God Uses
5) Activating My Due Season
6) Overcoming Divine Verdicts
7) The Outcome of Divine Wisdom
8) Understanding God's Restoration Mandate
9) Walking In the Victory and Authority of the Truth
10) God's Covenant Exemption
11) Destiny Restoration Pillars
12) Provoking Acceptable Praise
13) Understanding Divine Judgment
14) Activating Angelic Re-enforcement
15) Provoking Un-Merited Favo
16) The Benefits of the Speaking Faith
17) Understanding Divine Arrangement
18) How to Keep Your Healing
19) Understanding the Mysteries of the Speaking Faith
20) Understanding the Mysteries of Prophetic Healing
21) Operating Under the Rules of Creative Healing
22) Understanding the Joy of Breakthrough
23) Understanding the Mystery of Breakthrough
24) Understanding Divine Prosperity
25) Understanding Divine Healing
26) Retaining Your Inheritance
27) Overcoming Confusing Spirit
28) Commanding Angelic Escorts

29) Enforcing Your Inheritance In Christ Jesus
30) Understanding Your Guardian Angels
31) Overcoming the Dominion of Sin
32) Understanding the Voice of God
33) The Outstanding Benefits of the Anointing
34) The Audacity of the Blood of Jesus
35) Walking in the Reality of the Anointing
36) Escaping the Nightmare of Poverty
37) Understanding Your Harvest Season
38) Activating Your Success Buttons
39) Overcoming the Forces of Darkness
40) Overcoming the Devices of the Devil
41) Overcoming Demonic Agents
42) Overcoming the Sorrows of Failure
43) Rejecting the Sorrows of Failure
44) Resisting the Sorrows of Poverty
45) Restoring Broken Marriages
46) Redeeming Your Days
47) The Force of Vision
48) Overcoming the Forces of Ignorance
49) Understanding the Sacrifice of Small Beginning
50) The Might of Small Beginning
51) Understanding the Mysteries of Prophesy
52) Overcoming Dream Nightmares
53) Breaking the Shackles of the Curse of the Law
54) Understanding the Joy of Harvest
55) Wisdom for Signs & Wonders
56) Wisdom for Generational Impact
57) Wisdom for Marriage Stability
58) Understanding the Number of Your Days

59) Enforcing Your Kingdom Rights
60) Escaping the Traps of Immoralities
61) Escaping the Trap of Poverty
62) Accessing Biblical Prosperity
63) Accessing True Riches in Christ
64) Silencing the Voice of the Accuser
65) Overcoming the Forces of Oppositions
66) Quenching the Voice of the Avenger
67) Silencing Demonic Prediction & Projection
68) Silencing Your Mocker
69) Understanding the Power of the Holy Ghost
70) Understanding the Baptism of Power
71) The Mystery of the Blood of Jesus
72) Understanding the Mystery of Sanctification
73) Understanding the Power of Holiness
74) Understanding the Forces of Purity & Righteousness
75) Activating the Forces of Vengeance
76) Appreciating the Mystery of Restoration
77) Overcoming the Projection & Prediction of the Enemy
78) Engaging the Mystery of the Blood
79) Commanding the Power of the Speaking Faith
80) Uprooting the Forces Against Your Rising
81) Overcoming Mere Success Syndrome
82) Understanding Divine Sentence
83) Understanding the Mystery of Praise
84) Understanding the Author of Faith
85) The Mystery of the Finisher of Faith
86) Attracting Supernatural Favor

MIRACLE OF GOD MINISTRIES
NIGERIA CRUSADE
2012

MIRACLE OF GOD MINISTRIES
NIGERIA CRUSADE 2012

MIRACLE OF GOD MINISTRIES

NIGERIA CRUSADE

2012

MIRACLE OF GOD MINISTRIES

NIGERIA CRUSADE

2012

MIRACLE OF GOD MINISTRIES

NIGERIA CRUSADE 2012